SCIENCE IN ACTION
Energy: Making It Work

By Tom Johnston
Illustrated by Sarah Pooley

Gareth Stevens Publishing
Milwaukee

Library of Congress Cataloging-in-Publication Data

Johnston, Tom.
  Energy: making it work.

  (Science in action)
  Summary: Examines energy in its variety of forms, how one form of energy converts into another, and
alternative energy sources that may lie in the future.
  1. Power resources--Juvenile literature. 2. Force and energy--Juvenile literature. (1. Power resources. 2.
Force and energy) I. Pooley, Sarah, ill. II. Title. III. Series.
TJ163.23.J64 1988   J333.79   87-42751
ISBN 1-55532-430-4
ISBN 1-55532-405-3 (lib. bdg.)

North American edition first published in 1988 by
64190
Gareth Stevens, Inc.   7317 West Green Tree Road
Milwaukee, Wisconsin 53223, USA

This US edition copyright © 1988. First published as *Let's Imagine: Colour* in the United Kingdom by
The Bodley Head, London.

Text copyright ©1985 Tom Johnston
Illustrations copyright © 1985 Sarah Pooley

Hand lettering: Kathy Hall
Typeset by Web Tech, Milwaukee
Project editors: Mark Sachner and Rhoda Sherwood

Technical consultants: Jonathan Knopp, Chair, Science Department, Rufus King High School, Milwaukee;
Willette Knopp, Reading Specialist and Elementary Teacher, Fox Point-Bayside (Wis.) School District.

2 3 4 5 6 7 8 9 93 92 91 90 89 88

Energy is involved in everything we do and in everything that happens to us. We live in a vast sea of energy. Energy makes things work.

This energy has many different forms. Some forms are obvious because we use them to sense the world around us. Light, which we use in order to see, is one energy form. Sound, which we hear, is another. We can also feel energy with our skin when it is heated by a warm object. Movement and electricity are two other forms of energy that we use every day.

Some things have energy stored inside them. Sometimes this stored energy is like a wound-up elastic band that unwinds when we let go of it, or like a leaf that falls from a tree. We say these things had potential energy before they moved. At other times, the energy may be stored as chemical energy in, for example, oil, coal, and food.

Here are some easy experiments you can try to show how one form of energy can be "molded," or changed, into another. In each case, think about the kind of energy you start with and the kind you end up with.

5

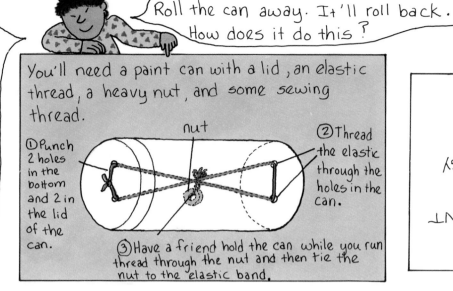

You and your friends can make a simple toy. It turns one energy form into another and back again. You could call it a boomerang can!

Roll the can away. It'll roll back. How does it do this?

You'll need a paint can with a lid, an elastic thread, a heavy nut, and some sewing thread.

nut

① Punch 2 holes in the bottom and 2 in the lid of the can.

② Thread the elastic through the holes in the can.

③ Have a friend hold the can while you run thread through the nut and then tie the nut to the elastic band.

ANSWER: IT TURNS MOVEMENT TO POTENTIAL (STORED) ENERGY AND BACK TO MOVEMENT AGAIN.

One of the energy forms that you use often is electricity. It is an easy form of energy to move, and it is fairly easy to mold into other energy forms.

The electrical energy in your house probably started off stored as chemical energy in oil or coal. This was burned at a power station to give electricity. When you turn on a switch at home, you then mold that electrical energy into other energy forms, such as light energy from a bulb or sound from a stereo.

We can also store electrical energy by turning it into chemical energy, to be reused when we need it. This is what a battery does.

A telephone turns sound energy into electrical energy, then back into sound again at the other end of the line.

Hi, Anna. It's George here.

Oh... hi, George. How are you?

Hm-m-m-m. George again!

We sometimes talk about energy when referring to people. You might say, about a girl who never sits still, "She's got lots of energy." Or you might say "I've got no energy left," as you collapse into a chair after a hard day at school. What you are really talking about is how much movement the person makes. And movement is a kind of energy.

So where does the energy come from that allows us to move around so much? From the food we eat. Food is really a store of chemical energy.

You may have seen commercials for food saying that they are low in calories. This is another way of saying they are low in energy. Scientists do not use *calorie* to measure the energy in food. They use a term from the metric system. They call a unit of energy a joule. One joule is about the amount of energy you need to carry an apple one yard or meter. One joule of energy is small, so we use kilojoule (KJ), which is 1,000 joules, when measuring energy. One calorie equals 4.184 KJ.

Different kinds of food contain different amounts of energy.

A ten-year-old needs about 2,400 calories (10,000 KJ) of energy a day, but the amount you need depends on how much exercise you do. Anyone who is overweight should not eat much fatty, high-energy food. Doctors worry that too many of these high-energy foods may cause people to have heart attacks later in life.

Magazines and books in health food stores often list the calories of energy that are in different foods. You could read one of these to try to figure out how much energy you are eating in a day. Many manufacturers put labels on their food to show the energy content.

We use food energy to move around and to keep our bodies warm.

Yes, but how did the energy get into the food in the first place?

Think about what you ate for breakfast. It may have been cereal made from corn or wheat with milk on it. The energy in the cereal came from the corn or wheat plant. The energy in the milk came from a cow. The cow got this energy in the first place by eating grass, a plant, and this plant contains mineral salts. Just about everything we eat, if we follow it back, has its energy source in the mineral salts plants take up from the soil through their roots.

Plants don't eat food to get their energy. They are made to collect light energy from the sun and store it as chemical energy inside themselves. This process of producing energy is called photosynthesis. So when you next eat French fries, remember that you are eating energy that was once light from the sun. There is a continuous natural flow of energy from the sun to plants and then to animals. And when animals die, their decaying bodies provide mineral salts for the plants again. We can see this flow through an energy web diagram.

SUN

SNAIL SLUG

BIRD

CAT

HUMAN

LETTUCE

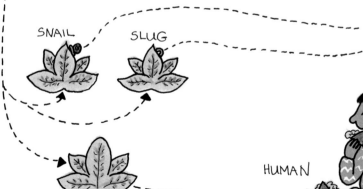

Look in your garden or a nearby waste site. Watch carefully! You'll see which animals are eating plants and which are eating other animals. Now draw up your own energy web!

10

THREE WAYS OUR BODIES KEEP WARM

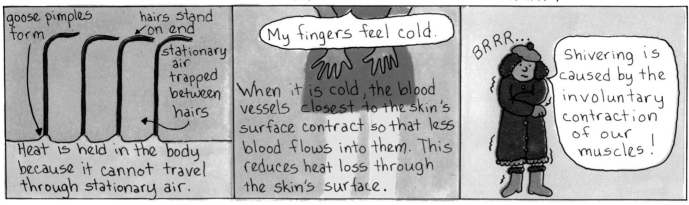

goose pimples form

hairs stand on end

stationary air trapped between hairs

Heat is held in the body because it cannot travel through stationary air.

My fingers feel cold.

When it is cold, the blood vessels closest to the skin's surface contract so that less blood flows into them. This reduces heat loss through the skin's surface.

BRRR...

Shivering is caused by the involuntary contraction of our muscles!

A lot of the energy that animals get from their food is lost from their bodies. The air around them, especially at night, is usually colder than they are. They lose energy to the colder air or anything else around them. If the animals were colder than the air, they would gain energy from it. This movement of energy is called heating.

Not only animals lose or gain energy like this. It can happen to any object, and it seems to happen in three different ways: conduction, convection, and radiation. There are lots of experiments you can do to see how heating takes place.

Premature and sick babies, accident victims, and people who are old are often wrapped in "survival" blankets when being transported to the hospital.

These blankets are like big pieces of foil which reflect a patient's body heat. Air pockets in the quilting add insulation. Survival blankets prevent energy loss, and this retained energy fights illness or shock.

The metal parts of my bike always feel colder than the plastic parts.

RING!

This is because the metal is better at taking the heating energy from my hands. Brrr.

Find something that is made of metal and plastic, such as a cooking pan or the handlebars of a bicycle. Touch the plastic part with one hand and the metal part with the other. Which part feels cooler?

You will find that the metal part feels cooler. This is because some of the energy is flowing out of your hand and into the metal. We call the way energy moves through the metal conduction. The plastic part does not conduct the energy away, so it feels warmer to the touch.

Here is another experiment to try:

Hold the ends of the spoons.

Which of my hands will feel warm first?

short metal spoon

bowl of hot water

long metal spoon

The hand with the short spoon feels warmer first because the energy did not have as far to travel. Eventually both hands are heated as both spoons conduct energy.

This experiment **must** be done outside, but away from the wind.

Be sure there's an adult nearby.

This kind of conduction happens in solids such as metals, which are the best conductors. Liquids and gases will not conduct energy.

In liquids and gases, the part that is being heated rises while the cooler part falls. The cooler and warmer air circulate in a process called convection. This simple experiment shows how it happens with a gas. Try it out.

Energy from the flame heats the air above it and this air rises.

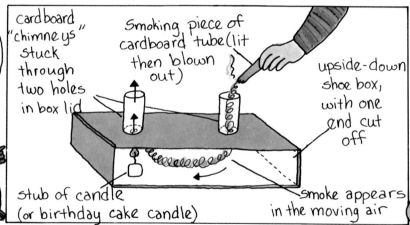

cardboard "chimneys" stuck through two holes in box lid

Smoking piece of cardboard tube (lit then blown out)

upside-down shoe box, with one end cut off

stub of candle (or birthday cake candle)

smoke appears in the moving air

Cooler air falls down the other side to replace the heated air. We call this circulation of energy convection.

If you try this experiment, you will see convection happen in a liquid.

The food coloring dyes the water, so you can see it moving.

drop of food coloring

water

jar

candle stub

The energy from the candle is making the water move.

As snug as a bug in a rug!

SUN

EARTH

The third way energy might move and produce a heating effect is by radiation. This is the way energy from the sun heats the earth. You can make a project that uses this radiated energy.

Make a triangular shape out of blackened cardboard and cut one side of it (as shown). Place your shape on a windowsill and hang a spiral of aluminum foil over the open end of your shape.

spiral of foil

SUN

Cut the spiral from a circle of foil

black cardboard

window

cool air

window sill

WATCH! As the sun shines, the black shape is heated and warms the air inside, which rises. The moving air spins the spiral shape.

A hot space heater gives out energy three ways to warm you up. The energy moves through the air by convection; it moves through anything solid that touches the heat source by conduction; and it moves out in all directions by radiation.

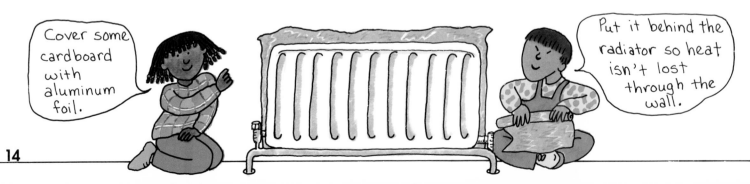

Cover some cardboard with aluminum foil.

Put it behind the radiator so heat isn't lost through the wall.

Here's an easy way to show this:

Imagine that a group of children are pretending to be molecules. Molecules are the tiny particles that everything is made of. The children are trying to "carry" energy from one place to heat up another place. Since we can't see energy, they are using water to represent it. They are trying to move the water from a bucket to a child sitting at the other end of the room.

15

If something is warm and you want to keep it that way, then you have to try to stop it from losing energy. Warm-blooded animals have fur or feathers to do this job for them. We must wear clothes.

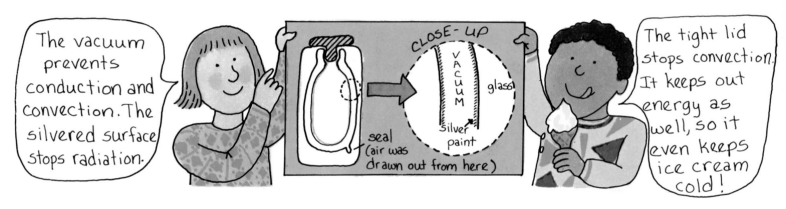

The vacuum prevents conduction and convection. The silvered surface stops radiation.

CLOSE-UP

glass

seal (air was drawn out from here)

silver paint

The tight lid stops convection. It keeps out energy as well, so it even keeps ice cream cold!

If you want to keep coffee hot, use a vacuum flask.

The vacuum flask keeps energy in or out because it is well insulated. In many countries, people must also insulate their homes to keep them warm inside. If you have a thermometer for measuring temperature you can see how this works.

① Take three identical glass jars.

② Put equal amounts of warm water into each jar.

③ Make lids for two jars: Put cotton between 2 pieces of cardboard.

thermometer

cotton layer between two pieces of cardboard

glass jar

warm water

box

* Be sure you read the thermometer while it is still in the water.

④ Make a hole in the center of the lid. Put one jar in a box.

⑤ Take the temperature of each at the start and after about half an hour.

⑥ Which one keeps warm the longest?

Our house hasn't got cavity walls or an insulated roof space. It's freezing!

Our house is well insulated - it even has double glazing on the windows! I'm as warm as toast in here.

Shiver me timbers!

The best-insulated houses have cavity walls — two layers of bricks with a gap between. This gap stops warm energy from being conducted through the wall. Energy can also escape upward by convection. Putting insulation in the roof space helps stop the air from moving.

If the snow on the roof doesn't melt, it means that a house is well insulated.

HOW TO MAKE A THERMOMETER

You'll need a plastic straw, some modeling clay to hold the straw, a narrow glass container, and some colored water.

Now heat your thermometer on a radiator. Watch the water rise up the straw.

Your thermometer works because as it gets warmer, the molecules of water gain energy. The molecules then move apart from each other and so the water expands (takes up more space). The hotter something is, the further up the tube the water will rise.

see-through plastic straw

modeling clay lump

colored water

glass container

17

Use your thermometer to measure lots of different temperatures.

A hot dog

To use your thermometer, you need to be able to see it. To read this book, you need to be able to see it. This involves using another important energy form, light.

By examining light, we can find out quite a few more things about energy.

As with most energy forms, light bounces off things. You see this happen when you use a mirror. To see it more clearly, try this experiment.

Light energy can also be made to bend. This happens when it moves from one substance to another, such as from water into air or air into glass. This gives a strange effect that you may have noticed before. When you look at things in water, for instance, they seem closer to you than they really are. This drawing shows why:

This bending of light is usually called refraction. This effect occurs in the lenses of microscopes, cameras, and binoculars. A lens is a shaped piece of glass. Some lenses, convex ones, curve outward and bend light inward. Other lenses, concave ones, curve inward and bend light outward. Convex lenses are used to get a picture on a screen. You find them in film projectors or in cameras. If you have a convex lens (a magnifying glass will do), try using it to get a picture like this:

20

Theodore H. Maiman invented the first operating laser.

He first demonstrated it in May 1960.

It is difficult to understand how light is a kind of energy unless we actually see it do some work. One spectacular example of light at work is the laser. Some lasers are powerful enough to punch holes through metal. A laser's light has even been bounced off the moon.

Laser stands for **l**ight **a**mplification by **s**timulated **e**mission of **r**adiation, which sounds hard to understand. Put more simply, a laser is a pure (one color), intense (very bright) beam of parallel light energy. "Parallel" means it doesn't spread out, but travels in a straight line.

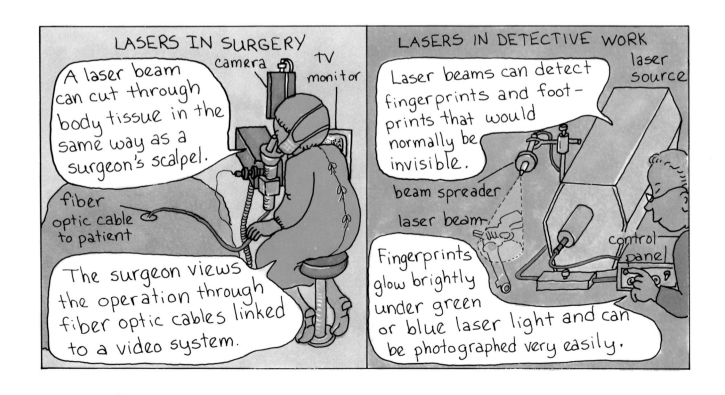

LASERS IN SURGERY

camera
tv monitor

A laser beam can cut through body tissue in the same way as a surgeon's scalpel.

fiber optic cable to patient

The surgeon views the operation through fiber optic cables linked to a video system.

LASERS IN DETECTIVE WORK

laser source

Laser beams can detect fingerprints and footprints that would normally be invisible.

beam spreader

laser beam

control panel

Fingerprints glow brightly under green or blue laser light and can be photographed very easily.

Lasers are now used in lots of ways. One of the most common is as bar code readers. Most products you can buy now have a series of black lines called a bar code printed on them. The codes are slightly different on different products. They can be read by a laser at the check-out counter of the store. This tells the computer-controlled cash register what the product is and how much it costs. The cash register then automatically gives a bill, checks how much of each thing is being sold, and re-orders it so that the store is kept stocked.

Lasers have also been used to read compact discs. These discs produce high quality sound. Some people predict that they will replace all other record and cassette sound systems.

Lasers are being used more in telephone systems, especially long distance ones. Here the laser light is carried along tiny tubes. Lasers have also been used in printing, in hospitals for specialized surgery, and in military guidance systems. Thankfully, however, laser weapons have not yet been mass-produced.

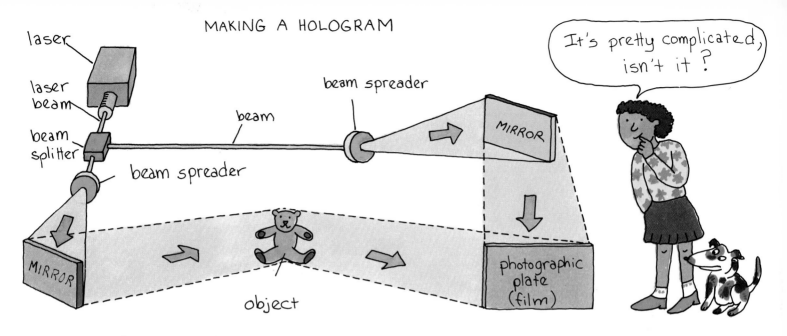

Lasers are also used to produce holograms, three-dimensional images that seem to float in the air. This means that you can look at them from any direction, just as you can real images.

Holograms are made when a laser beam splits. One beam hits a mirror and then the photographic plate. The other hits a mirror, travels to the object to be filmed, and moves on to the photographic plate. Later, a laser shone through this film produces the 3-D image.

Some other energy waves from the sun that would be harmful to us are kept out by a layer of ozone gas high in the atmosphere.

You can't get suntanned behind a window. It lets light and heat through, but not ultra-violet rays.

The ozone layer is like Earth's window!

But we have not yet mentioned all the forms energy can take. The sun's rays, for example, take three forms: ultraviolet ("beyond" violet), infrared ("below" red), and visible light. The ultraviolet rays give the sun tan, the infrared cause heating, and the visible rays are the ones we see.

To show how similar infrared rays are to light energy, we can shine sunlight through a prism. This breaks the light energy into colors. Each color has a slightly different amount of energy. Just below the red end of the sunlight would be infrared.

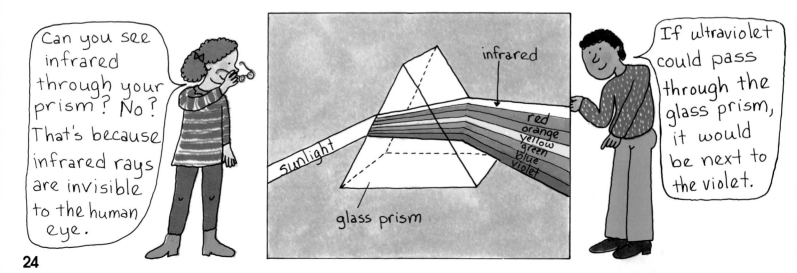

Can you see infrared through your prism? No? That's because infrared rays are invisible to the human eye.

infrared

sunlight

red
orange
yellow
green
blue
violet

glass prism

If ultraviolet could pass through the glass prism, it would be next to the violet.

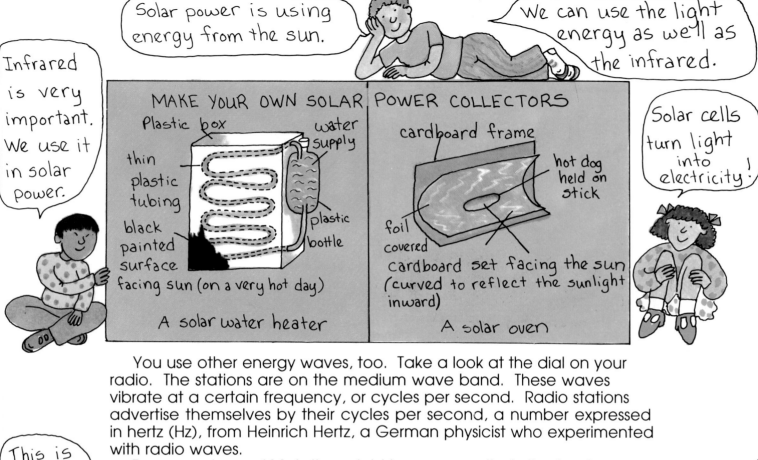

Solar power is using energy from the sun.

We can use the light energy as well as the infrared.

Infrared is very important. We use it in solar power.

Solar cells turn light into electricity!

MAKE YOUR OWN SOLAR POWER COLLECTORS

Plastic box
water supply
thin plastic tubing
black painted surface facing sun (on a very hot day)
plastic bottle

A solar water heater

cardboard frame
hot dog held on stick
foil covered cardboard set facing the sun (curved to reflect the sunlight inward)

A solar oven

You use other energy waves, too. Take a look at the dial on your radio. The stations are on the medium wave band. These waves vibrate at a certain frequency, or cycles per second. Radio stations advertise themselves by their cycles per second, a number expressed in hertz (Hz), from Heinrich Hertz, a German physicist who experimented with radio waves.

For example, an AM station might have waves that vibrate at the frequency of 1,020,000Hz. But writing this long hertz number, plus the hertz for other stations in your city, would take up a lot of space on the dial. So we use kilohertz (KHz). This is 1,000 hertz. The station, then, would be found at 1020KHz on the AM dial.

FM stations have waves that vibrate even more times per second, so their station number is expressed in megahertz (MHz). This is a million hertz. A station at 90MHz on your FM dial has radio waves traveling at the frequency of 90,000,000Hz.

This is KDKA in Pittsburgh, PA, transmitting on 1020 KHz

Hey. Turn the knob! I want some real music!

FM	88	92	96	100	104	106	108		MHz
AM	540	600		700	800	1000	1200	1400	1600	KHz

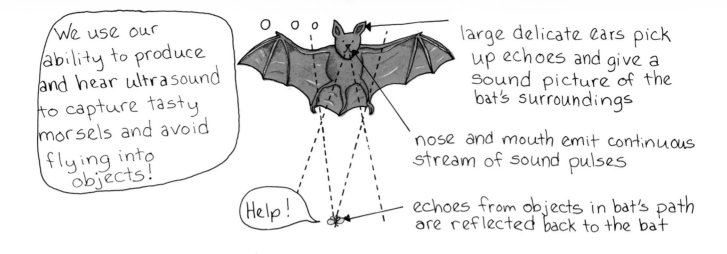

But we don't hear the radio waves. They are turned into sound energy for us by the radio. We pick up sound waves that are between 20Hz and 20,000Hz, although when we are young, we generally have better high-frequency hearing. Anything faster than 20,000Hz we call ultrasound. Some creatures, such as bats and dolphins, can produce and hear ultrasound. If you go outside on a quiet night, you might just hear a bat call at the extreme range of your hearing. Although we can't hear ultrasound, it is still useful. Hospitals use ultrasound machines to "see" babies while they are still inside their mother. They give us pictures a little like X-rays, which are another form of energy.

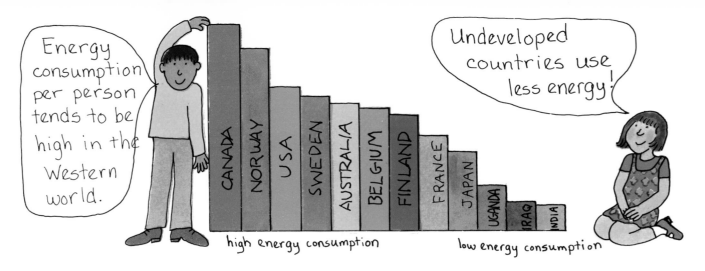

Many people are worried that we may shortly face a world energy crisis. We are using up chemical stores of energy such as oil, gas, and coal too quickly. These may last a few hundred years longer, but no more than that. In fact, we could become seriously low on oil during your lifetime.

NUCLEAR FISSION

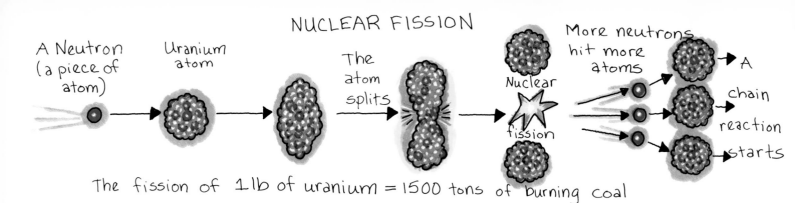

A Neutron (a piece of atom) → Uranium atom → The atom splits → Nuclear fission → More neutrons hit more atoms → A chain reaction starts

The fission of 1 lb of uranium = 1500 tons of burning coal

In many parts of the world, people are trying to use energy directly from the sun and from wind and water. Nuclear power stations use uranium to produce energy. Nuclear reactors smash apart atoms (tiny particles within molecules), which lets out the energy inside the atoms. This is called nuclear fission. Some people don't want to do this. Nuclear fission produces dangerous radioactive waste that can kill living things. Even if using nuclear fission power becomes more widespread, it won't solve all our energy problems. Even uranium will run out one day.

Albert Einstein 1879 – 1955

Albert Einstein predicted in 1905 that a little amount of any substance could in theory be changed to a large amount of energy.

Einstein's prediction came true when nuclear energy was produced, but he could never have imagined how it was to be used...

On August 6, 1945, the US dropped an atom bomb on the city of Hiroshima, Japan. It brought an end to World War II.

It destroyed the city and killed 80,000 people. Many more were to die later from radiation sickness.

But there is another source of energy — nuclear fusion. It uses the same principle as the sun itself to make larger atoms from smaller ones. Exposed to the sun, hydrogen is turned into helium, and helium gives out vast amounts of energy. Scientists are working now to try to harness this energy source.

In the future, we will get our energy from many sources. These may include some large power stations, perhaps nuclear fusion ones, and a variety of sources that can be renewed. So depending on where you live, your energy could be supplied from wind or water turbines, solar cells, or tidal power generators.

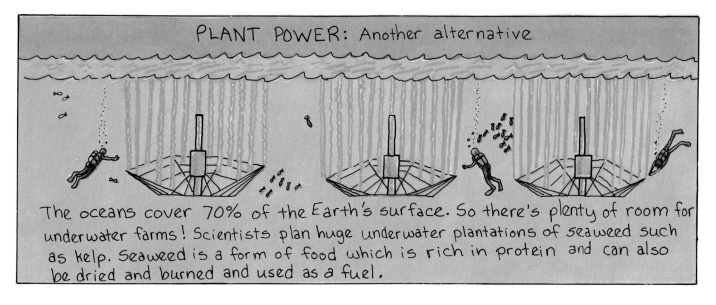

PLANT POWER: Another alternative

The oceans cover 70% of the Earth's surface. So there's plenty of room for underwater farms! Scientists plan huge underwater plantations of seaweed such as kelp. Seaweed is a form of food which is rich in protein and can also be dried and burned and used as a fuel.

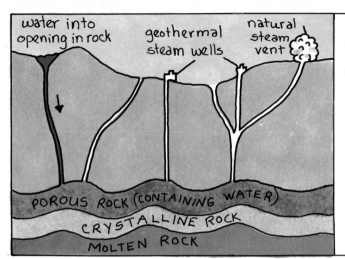

GEOTHERMAL ENERGY

Beneath the Earth's crust is a central core estimated to be 8,500°F (4,700°C). This molten rock heats the layers above it. Water trickling through porous rock is heated and turned into steam. Geothermal wells can tap either the steam vents or the hot water in the porous rock. The steam can be used to drive turbo-generators and the water for heating.

We must also lower the amount of energy we use. There are many ways to do this: We can use better insulation in our houses, and we can wear warmer clothes when it is cold rather than turn up the heat. Private cars could become a thing of the past, since energy is used more efficiently if people travel on public transportation such as buses and trains. We can also use bicycles to get around.

Solar collectors in space

Hydroelectric power station (producing electricity from water)

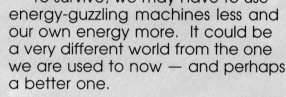

Wave-energy collectors bob up and down off the coast

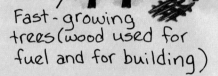

Fast-growing trees (wood used for fuel and for building)

Nuclear fusion power station

To survive, we may have to use energy-guzzling machines less and our own energy more. It could be a very different world from the one we are used to now — and perhaps a better one.

Windmills provide energy for heat and light and for pumping water

Dome-shaped houses (the most energy-saving shape)

roof solar panels

well-insulated interior

Our diet would rely more on raw food

Solar panels for heating collected rainwater

Warm insulated clothing

Glossary

Calorie: a unit of heat. It tells us how much heat energy we obtain from foods and lose during exercise.

Conduction: the passage of heat energy through a solid such as metal.

Conductor: a material that carries heat or electrical energy.

Convection: a circular process of transferring heat; in this process, heat energy passes through a fluid such as water or a gas such as air.

Heat: the form of energy released through conduction, convection, or radiation.

Hertz: the cycles per second, or frequency, that a radio wave vibrates.

Infrared light: light whose waves are longer than the waves of visible light and shorter than microwaves.

Joule: a unit of measurement that tells how much energy is required to move an object a certain distance.

Nuclear fission: the process of splitting the nucleus of an atom into fragments; this releases nuclear energy.

Nuclear fusion: the process of fusing or joining the nuclei of atoms to create larger nuclei and to release nuclear energy.

Photosynthesis: a process that plants perform, making food from the carbon dioxide in sunlight and also releasing oxygen into the air.

Potential energy: energy that is stored in an object, waiting to be acted upon and released.

Radiation: the process of passing light, sound, and heat energy through the air.

Reflection: the process of bouncing light, sound, and heat energy off an object.

Refraction: the bending of a wave of light or sound as it crosses the boundary between substances of different density — for example, the boundary between air and water.

Ultraviolet light: invisible light waves that are just beyond the violet rays of visible light.

Index